THE ART OF DISAPPEARING

Stephanie Alison Walker

I0139730

BROADWAY PLAY PUBLISHING INC
New York
www.broadwayplaypublishing.com
info@broadwayplaypublishing.com

Cover art by Arlene Warner

First edition: September 2022
I S B N: 978-0-88145-941-8

Book design: Marie Donovan
Page make-up: Adobe InDesign
Typeface: Palatino

THE ART OF DISAPPEARING was first produced at 16th Street Theater (Ann Filmer, Artistic Director) in Berwyn, Illinois, from 22 January-28 February 2015. The cast and creative contributors were:

CHARLOTTE .... Joan Kohn
HENRY .... Tom McElroy
MELISSA/SECURITY GUARD .... Amanda Powell
JACK/DOCTOR .... Andrés Enriquez

Director .... Ann Filmer
Original music & sound design .... Barry Bennett
Properties design .... Jesse Gaffney
Scenic design .... Joanna Iwanicka
Costume design .... Rachel S Parent
Light design .... Cat Wilson

CHARACTERS & SETTING

MELISSA, *26, struggling artist. Headstrong with something to prove.*

CHARLOTTE, *56,* MELISSA*'s mother. A woman who can hold a grudge.*

HENRY, *57,* MELISSA*'s father. Owner of a sign company. Confrontation avoider.*

JACK, *30s,* MELISSA*'s friend. Gallery owner. The one person who believes in her art. A "good guy".*

DOCTOR, *30s, played by the same actor who plays* JACK.

SECURITY GUARD, *played by the same actress as* MELISSA.

MELISSA*'s tiny apartment in an "up-and-coming" neighborhood of Chicago /* HENRY *and* CHARLOTTE*'s house in an affluent suburb on the north shore of Chicago / and various other settings*

Time: Spring 2009

For my Grandma Eileen and those who loved her

ACT ONE

Scene 1

(Sunday brunch. HENRY *and* CHARLOTTE'*s kitchen.)*

(At rise:)

(Lights up on HENRY *and* CHARLOTTE'*s kitchen where* MELISSA *[26] sits looking at* JACK *[30] who takes in the surroundings while* HENRY *[56] pours coffee.)*

*(*HENRY *pours a good amount of milk in his cup.* MELISSA *watches.)*

HENRY: *(Off* MELISSA'*s look)* It cuts the acidity.

MELISSA: You never take cream in your coffee.

HENRY: I do now. Have. For a while, actually.

MELISSA: You always told me to drink it black. *(Imitating* HENRY*)* "If you must drink coffee, drink it black."

HENRY: I know.

MELISSA: No sugar, no cream. Black. Just black.

HENRY: Yeah, well. Doctor's orders.

(Off MELISSA'*s look again:)*

HENRY: Ulcer.

MELISSA: Oh.

(Beat)

(HENRY *sits and wraps both hands around his steaming mug of coffee.*)

HENRY: *(To* JACK*)* So, Jason—

JACK: Jack.

MELISSA: His name's Jack.

HENRY: That's right. Jack. What, uh, what is it you do?

MELISSA: He's a gallery owner.

HENRY: Oh. What kind of gallery?

JACK: Art. Modern art.

HENRY: A business owner already at your age. Impressive.

JACK: It's actually, technically my father's gallery.

MELISSA: But Jack's being groomed to take the business over because his father's retiring.

HENRY: Family business. That's good. Good for you, Jack. Is that how you know each other then? The gallery?

JACK: Yes, sir.

MELISSA: So formal. You can call him Henry.

(JACK *looks to* HENRY *for approval.*)

HENRY: Sure. Yes. Call me Henry. So you met at the gallery?

MELISSA: Yes.

JACK: Actually, I met you at the coffee shop.

MELISSA: We met at the gallery.

JACK: *(To* HENRY*)* It was at the coffee shop. It was love at first sight. For me.

HENRY: Oh, well let's hear it.

JACK: I was reading *Walden*. Well, re-reading. See I, uh, never paid attention in high school. Never took it seriously. So now that I actually care, I feel like I'm somehow incomplete until I re-read everything I read as a teenager.

HENRY: Huh.

JACK: Dostoevsky's next on my list. *The Brothers K.* I figure that should take me through the winter months. Anyway, I'm in this coffee shop getting bored with Thoreau because, let's face it, it's not *all* fascinating. The guy goes on and on about clothes. I didn't remember that at all. He just catalogues clothes. What is that?

HENRY: No idea.

MELISSA: Jack.

JACK: Anyway, I get up to get another cup of coffee and that's when I see her- hanging in a dark corner - all alone and vulnerable. A gut-wrenching display of beauty and rage...utterly raw yet somehow shy...and above all—desperately wanting to be understood. I just stared. Openly. For minutes.

HENRY: Uh...

MELISSA: He's talking about my painting, Dad.

HENRY: Oh. Oh! Okay. Huh.

JACK: I'm a fourth generation art dealer.... I can't help but sound like a prick sometimes when I talk about a painting.

MELISSA: You don't sound like a prick.

HENRY: Well...

MELISSA: Dad.

HENRY: Maybe just a little.

MELISSA: Dad!

HENRY: I'm kidding. I just had no idea what he was talking about. That's all. *(To JACK)* That's all. Continue.

JACK: It's just…that was the moment for me. I got my coffee and went back to Thoreau but kept re-reading the same page. I finally gave in and went home. Thinking about her. I spent a lot of time thinking about this one. It got inside of me…and I couldn't quite figure out why. It's not that it was technically brilliant or significant—

MELISSA: Hey—

JACK: What? We've talked about this before. *(To HENRY)* I have to be honest. I refuse to blow smoke up any artist's…you know. Because it doesn't help them.

HENRY: Sure.

JACK: I went back and bought it. For myself. Which I never do. But I did. So obviously I was deeply impacted by your work. By the hope the need and the promise. I got Melissa's e-mail from the coffee shop owner. E-mailed her. Invited her to the gallery. She was not what I expected, but also not a surprise.

MELISSA: Gee, thanks.

JACK: I only mean to say that you, like your work, are a walking contradiction. *(He's never told her this.)* You make people want to discover your soul.

(MELISSA is speechless.)

HENRY: That's…wow.

(HENRY shakes JACK's hand vigorously.)

MELISSA: Dad.

HENRY: It's a nice story. *(Beat)* Your mother would like that story.

MELISSA: No, she wouldn't.

(Beat)

JACK: So, uh, Melissa said you own a sign company?

HENRY: Yep.

JACK: Like billboards?

HENRY: No, no. Custom commercial signage. Schools, theaters, churches, banks... You know the marquee for the Loop Theatre?

JACK: Yeah. Sure.

HENRY: Our's.

JACK: Do you do smaller jobs, like say signage for a small art gallery?

HENRY: Sure. Just...

(HENRY reaches into his pocket and pulls out a card. Hands it to JACK.)

JACK: Great. I'll, uh—

HENRY: Yeah, just give me a call.

JACK: Good. I will.

(A beat. MELISSA looks around the room.)

MELISSA: You redecorated.

HENRY: Hmm?

MELISSA: It's brighter.

HENRY: Oh yeah. That was...a while ago. Your mother wanted a change.

MELISSA: I liked it better before.

(A beat)

HENRY: So when, uh, when is the wedding? Have you set a date?

MELISSA: We're just enjoying being engaged, right sweetie? *(She gives JACK a look.)*

JACK: Right. Sweetie.

HENRY: Well, I know it's been a long time, but... it is still a, a surprise.

JACK: I know!

MELISSA: We're very happy.

(A beat. The moment's tense.)

HENRY: I suppose congratulations are in order.

JACK: That's not necessary.

MELISSA: Of course it is.

(HENRY raises his coffee mug for a toast.)

HENRY: *(Unconvincing)* To the, the, to the...bride and groom...to be.

(They toast. They sip the coffee.)

(A beat. Everyone collectively sips their coffee. MELISSA watches the stairs.)

HENRY: It's so good to see you, Melissa. Such a nice surprise.

MELISSA: Why didn't Mom tell you I was coming?

HENRY: You look happy.

MELISSA: *(Defensive)* I am happy.

HENRY: Good. I'm glad.

MELISSA: Are you happy?

HENRY: Uh, sure.

MELISSA: Good. I'm glad.

HENRY: Could always be happier, though, right?

JACK: Never can be too happy.

(MELISSA gives JACK a look.)

JACK: I mean. That's what they say. Whatever.

HENRY: It's true. And a parent always hopes for the most happiness for their children.

MELISSA: I am happy, Dad. Okay?

HENRY: Okay.

MELISSA: Besides, nobody is happy all the time. And if they are, they're lying or they're delusional.

HENRY: I don't know about that.

MELISSA: You don't? You think it's possible to be happy all the time?

HENRY: I don't know. But I do want YOU to be happy. That's not a crime.

(JACK *awkwardly stands.*)

MELISSA: *(To* JACK*)* What are you doing?

JACK: Oh, I was just thinking...I have phone call I completely forgot about. I'll just step out front and let you two you know—father daughter...catch up...and, you know...

MELISSA: No. We're leaving.

HENRY: What? No. You just got here.

MELISSA: Dad—

HENRY: You want to go out? Get some brunch? Just don't leave yet. Please. You came this far. You may as well finish your coffee.

(MELISSA *considers.*)

JACK: I'm just gonna be out front.

(JACK *brushes past* MELISSA. *She grabs his arm to stop him.*)

MELISSA: Jack—

(JACK *looks at* MELISSA, *leans in and kisses her gently on the cheek—she turns her head away.*

JACK: *(While exiting)* Just yell if you need me. *(He is gone.)*

(A long beat)

HENRY: Seems like a good guy. How long have you two been—?

MELISSA: *(Beat)* Jack's curating a show of my work at his gallery. My very own show.

HENRY: So you're still painting, then?

MELISSA: Yes, I'm still painting, Dad.

HENRY: Good. That's good. I'm glad to hear it's working out.

MELISSA: I'm working on a big commission right now.

HENRY: Commission? So, you're getting paid?

MELISSA: Always about the money.

HENRY: No, I'm just... *(Beat)* That's great. Who's it for?

MELISSA: What?

HENRY: The commission...

MELISSA: Oh. Uh, the mayor.

HENRY: The mayor?! Wow!

MELISSA: Well, his wife. The mayor's wife.

HENRY: Still. The mayor's wife. That's just great. Must be a huge boost for your career. Good for you, Melissa.

MELISSA: You can officially tell Mom she was wrong about me...whatever that's worth. I would tell her myself, but...

HENRY: She didn't mention anything about a brunch.

MELISSA: She invited me!

HENRY: It just seems strange that she wouldn't mention it.

MELISSA: You think I'd just show up out the blue expecting brunch. Just like that? For no reason?

HENRY: She called you?

MELISSA: Yes. It was very strange. She sounded...kind.

HENRY: And you're sure it was for this Sunday?

MELISSA: I'm sure. Why won't she come downstairs?

HENRY: It's not...I didn't... can we just. Let's just have a father daughter thing here.

MELISSA: Thing?

HENRY: Moment. Breakfast.

MELISSA: *(Calling off)* Mom?!

HENRY: Melissa.

MELISSA: I'm going up there.

HENRY: She's—

MELISSA: In the tub? *(She stands.)*
(She turns and charges the stairs. She's up them in a few swift bounds.)

HENRY: Honey—!

(HENRY watches the stairs for several beats. Silence. MELISSA walks slowly back down. He stands. She gets to the bottom and faces him.)

MELISSA: She's not in the tub.

HENRY: Now, I did say that/

MELISSA: She's not even here.

HENRY: /I didn't know anything about a brunch.

MELISSA: *(Exiting)* I'm such an idiot.

HENRY: Melissa—

(MELISSA is gone. Lights shift as HENRY sinks into his chair.)

Scene 2

(An hour later. HENRY *contemplates his coffee as if he hasn't moved a muscle since* MELISSA *left. He looks up as* CHARLOTTE, 56, *enters. She is full of energy and life.)*

CHARLOTTE: I feel like a new woman!

*(*CHARLOTTE *kisses* HENRY *on the cheek and shows him her freshly painted nails.)*

CHARLOTTE: Just natural. They look pretty, don't they? *(She goes to the fridge and gets a bottle of water.)* Cindy wasn't there today. I had the new girl for my massage. She's a lot stronger than she looks. And a talker. She didn't stop talking the entire time. Apparently she just got back from hiking the entire Appalachian Trail. *(She looks at* HENRY.*)* Are you listening to me?

HENRY: Huh? Yeah. Appalachian Trail.

CHARLOTTE: I guess it's quite the transcendental experience. It's just over two thousand miles. Can you imagine that? Walking over two thousand miles? It took her almost six months to complete. Nothing but walking for six whole months. Georgia to Maine. No thank you. *(She stops to take a sip of water.)* Anyway, she was telling me this story about one of her many miracles along the way. They call them miracles. It's when you ask the universe for something and it provides. Like magic. One time, she was telling me, she had a craving for an icy cold Budweiser. For days. Days and days all she could think about was Budweiser. She's a beer drinker. I think she might be a lesbian, actually. Anyway, she's in the woods... hot, tired and craving a Bud. But it's not like she can stop by at the corner bar for a beer when she's walking in the woods, right? She was really far from any sort of civilization at this point. Can you believe that? That it's actually possible to get away from civilization nowadays? So there she is in the woods and after hours of thinking about nothing but that beer, she suddenly sees something on the trail ahead of her. Do you know what it was?

(Beat. No response.)

CHARLOTTE: Henry?

HENRY: What?

CHARLOTTE: Do you know what she saw?

HENRY: A bear?

CHARLOTTE: No. Not a bear. A six-pack of Budweiser. Just sitting there. As if it was waiting for her. And it was cold.

(CHARLOTTE looks to HENRY for a response. Nothing)

CHARLOTTE: Evidently things like that happen all the time on the trail. There are these people called "trail angels" that will leave gifts on the trail for the hikers. Isn't that fascinating?

(No response)

CHARLOTTE: Henry.

HENRY: Huh?

CHARLOTTE: I said, "Isn't that fascinating?"

HENRY: Oh. Yes.

CHARLOTTE: You weren't even listening, were you?

HENRY: I experienced a sort of miracle myself this morning.

CHARLOTTE: Did you? What happened?

(A beat)

HENRY: Our daughter came home for brunch.

(Another beat)

CHARLOTTE: I'm sorry. What?

HENRY: The doorbell rang around ten and there she was.

CHARLOTTE: *(After a beat)* She wanted money, didn't she?

HENRY: She said you invited her. To brunch.

CHARLOTTE: Brunch.

HENRY: That's what she said.

CHARLOTTE: I didn't invite her to brunch. I haven't even talked to her in...

HENRY: Two years.

CHARLOTTE: Has it been that long?

HENRY: If you can believe it.

CHARLOTTE: She must need something. She didn't ask you for help? For money?

HENRY: No, no. She was here for brunch. That's all.

CHARLOTTE: No. She wants something from us. You'll see.

HENRY: I don't think so.

CHARLOTTE: Then why? Why now?

HENRY: I don't know. Maybe because she's getting married and—

CHARLOTTE: Married?

HENRY: Yes. She brought her fiancé.

CHARLOTTE: Married.

HENRY: Evidently.

(Silence. Then)

CHARLOTTE: What's he like?

HENRY: Seems nice. I don't know. What do you want me to say? I hadn't seen our daughter in years and she shows up out of the blue. I wasn't really paying attention to the fiancé. *(Beat)* So you didn't invite her?

CHARLOTTE: No, Henry. I didn't invite her.

HENRY: *(A beat)* I just don't know what motive Melissa would have to lie. And she was genuinely upset that you weren't here. She thought you purposely invited her and then didn't show up.

CHARLOTTE: Purposely? For what purpose, exactly?

HENRY: I don't know. She was so angry. So...

CHARLOTTE: What? So what?

HENRY: Never mind. I just miss her, Charlotte, okay?

CHARLOTTE: You think I don't?

HENRY: I didn't say that. It was seeing her. Seeing her made me realize...

CHARLOTTE: Made you realize what, Henry? What?

HENRY: That I miss her and—

CHARLOTTE: Did she apologize?

(No response)

CHARLOTTE: Did she apologize, Henry?

HENRY: No. No she did not.

(A long beat. HENRY watches CHARLOTTE. CHARLOTTE drinks her water.)

HENRY: Honestly, is that really so important after all this time?

(No answer)

HENRY: She's our daughter.

(No answer)

HENRY: Charlotte?

(No answer)

HENRY: Charlotte?

(CHARLOTTE *finally turns and looks at* HENRY.)

CHARLOTTE: What was I saying? Oh, right. She's a beer drinker. I think she might be a lesbian, actually.

HENRY: What are you…

CHARLOTTE: She's in the woods…hot, tired and craving a Bud. She's really far from any sort of civilization at this point. And after hours of thinking about nothing but that beer, a six-pack of Budweiser materializes on the trail in front of her—

HENRY: (*Interrupting*) The Budweiser was cold. A "trail angel" had left it for her.

(*A beat*)

CHARLOTTE: I'm impressed. You were listening.

(*Lights. End of Scene*)

Scene 3

(*Lights up on* MELISSA's *studio apartment as* MELISSA *and* JACK *enter.*)

(MELISSA *crosses to her bedroom area and goes directly behind the room divider.*)

JACK: I shouldn't have said anything. I'm sorry.

MELISSA: Close the door, Jack.

(JACK *closes and locks the door.*)

JACK: I didn't mean to overstep—

MELISSA: You didn't overstep.

JACK: (*Carefully choosing his words*) But I can see that I upset you. And I'm sorry. That wasn't my intention. I really do apologize.

(MELISSA *steps out from behind the room divider in her painting jeans and a bra.*)

MELISSA: Stop apologizing.

(Beat)

JACK: But—

MELISSA: No. Jesus. You're acting like I'm some overly sensitive…female. Or something.

JACK: That's not what I meant to convey—

MELISSA: Oh, for fuck sake, Jack!

JACK: What?

MELISSA: Stop calculating every word. Just say what you want to say.

JACK: You lied.

MELISSA: About what?

JACK: Everything.

MELISSA: Not everything.

JACK: You should've told me you were gonna pawn me off as your fiancee. I could've used a little warning.

MELISSA: Oh, you loved it.

(JACK *just looks at* MELISSA.)

MELISSA: I don't know why I said it.

JACK: It was incredibly awkward. I'm a terrible liar.

MELISSA: You're an amazing liar. That story about the painting.

JACK: Well that wasn't a lie, was it?

MELISSA: It was the context that was a lie. The part about falling in love with me—with my painting with wanting to discover my soul…and… *(Looking at* JACK) It just slipped out. I'm sorry. I didn't intend on turning you into a liar. I am sorry. Just please don't look at me like that.

JACK: Like what?

MELISSA: Like you're disappointed in me.

JACK: That's not it.

MELISSA: I know that look.

(MELISSA *sits.* JACK *sits. A beat*)

JACK: I thought your dad was nice.

MELISSA: Nice. Nice. Such a blah word.

JACK: What I meant—

MELISSA: No. It's fitting. He's blah. No backbone there. Ol' Henry, the devoted husband. Ol' Henry, the C E O. Blah. Blah. Blah.

(MELISSA *grabs a T-shirt off the changing screen and pulls it over her head.* JACK *just watches. A beat*)

JACK: I should go.

(MELISSA *starts setting up her art supplies.*)

MELISSA: You got plans or something?

JACK: What?

MELISSA: Hot date?

JACK: Oh. I don't know. No. You gonna work?

MELISSA: What can I say? I'm inspired.

JACK: Good. That's good because my father has been asking to see something exemplary of what you want to show.

MELISSA: I know.

JACK: So…

MELISSA: What?

JACK: Put it all on the canvas.

(MELISSA *just looks at* JACK.)

JACK: But you know that. I'm just gonna…

MELISSA: I am trying, you know. To… "put it all on the canvas." It's just such an easy thing to say and…

JACK: I have faith in you.

(*This steals* MELISSA*'s breath for a moment.*)

JACK: Well…I'll let you…

MELISSA: Okay.

(JACK *starts to go.*)

MELISSA: Wait!

JACK: What?

MELISSA: Well, you don't happen to know the mayor's wife, do you?

JACK: The mayor. Like the mayor of Chicago?

MELISSA: Yeah. Never mind. It's stupid.

JACK: My father knows her.

MELISSA: He does?

JACK: Why?

MELISSA: Well, in that case…I need you…to get her…to commission a painting from me.

(*End of scene*)

Scene 4

(*Lights up on* HENRY *reading in bed—with the help of reading glasses.*)

CHARLOTTE: (*O S*) Henry! Henry!

HENRY: I'm in bed, Charlotte.

(CHARLOTTE *enters in her nightgown and robe. She's holding an empty bottle of prescription pills.*)

CHARLOTTE: She did it again! My pills are missing!

(CHARLOTTE *shakes the bottle upside down to demonstrate. HENRY puts his book down. Takes off his reading glasses*)

CHARLOTTE: Henry!

HENRY: Okay. Let's just calm down.

CHARLOTTE: I will not calm down! My pills are missing.

HENRY: Your pills?

CHARLOTTE: My Ambien.

HENRY: Your Ambien?

CHARLOTTE: Yes, Henry. My Ambien. My sleeping pills!

HENRY: Charlotte—

CHARLOTTE: How am I supposed to sleep tonight?

HENRY: Take a moment. Deep breath.

CHARLOTTE: Don't do that. Don't calm me down. I will not calm down.

HENRY: Okay. (*He puts his reading glasses back on and picks up his book.*)

CHARLOTTE: Last night I had a full bottle of Ambien. And now... (*She shakes the bottle upside down again.*) Empty. How do you explain that?

HENRY: (*In his book*) I don't know. Maybe you were mistaken.

CHARLOTTE: You know perfectly well what happened.

HENRY: It's late, Charlotte.

CHARLOTTE: It's late? How is that an answer to anything?

HENRY: Just come to bed.

CHARLOTTE: You know I can't sleep without my Ambien.

HENRY: Yes you can.

CHARLOTTE: No. I can't.

HENRY: Okay.

CHARLOTTE: I just want my pills back. I won't be mad. I won't press charges. Though I could.

HENRY: You're talking about our daughter.

CHARLOTTE: Call her and get them back, Henry.

HENRY: I'm not going to do that.

CHARLOTTE: This is your fault. You have to fix it.

(HENRY *puts the book back down.*)

HENRY: My fault?

CHARLOTTE: You let her in the house.

HENRY: Charlotte, I really think you need to take a step back and—

CHARLOTTE: Don't talk to me like I'm a child.

HENRY: First of all, Melissa wasn't up here. She was with me in the kitchen the whole time. She didn't even use the bathroom.

CHARLOTTE: That you saw. I mean, you're not the most observant person, Henry. Just get my pills back.

HENRY: Tomorrow morning we'll just go to the pharmacy and get some more. Okay?

CHARLOTTE: How am I supposed to sleep tonight?!

HENRY: I don't know. Try counting sheep.

CHARLOTTE: This isn't funny, Henry. She hasn't changed. My pills are missing on the same day she was in our house after years of not setting foot in our house…when she last stole my pills. It's not a coincidence! Wake up!

(HENRY *doesn't respond. Instead, he again removes his reading glasses and places them on the bedside table.*)

CHARLOTTE: What about the fiancé? They could be in this together.

(HENRY *rolls away from* CHARLOTTE. *He's done.*)

CHARLOTTE: What do you think happened to my pills then, Henry? Some random criminal broke in and took only my Ambien?

(HENRY *reaches over and turns the light off.*)

CHARLOTTE: What are you doing, Henry? I'm not finished. Henry!

(*No response.* CHARLOTTE *storms off.*)

(*End of scene*)

Scene 5

(MELISSA's *studio apartment. 7 A M*)

(*Lights up on* MELISSA *in her bathrobe with* HENRY *who is dressed in a business suit and holding two "to go" cups of coffee.*)

HENRY: Morning.

MELISSA: Coffee?

HENRY: For you.

(HENRY *hands* MELISSA *the coffee, she waits a beat, then takes it, turns and crosses towards her kitchen table.*)

MELISSA: It's still dark out.

HENRY: I thought you'd be up. Getting ready for work.

(MELISSA *sits at the table.*)

(HENRY *closes and locks the door.*)

MELISSA: I was out.

HENRY: You were out?

MELISSA: Of coffee. I was just gonna make some, but… I'm out. And then you show up with coffee.

HENRY: How fortuitous.

MELISSA: Eerie. Like you planned it or something.

HENRY: *(Beat)* So this is where you live.

MELISSA: How did you know?

HENRY: It's not a secret, is it?

MELISSA: No. I just…I didn't know you knew where I lived.

HENRY: Jack told me. *(Off her look)* He called me about his gallery's signage.

MELISSA: Did he?

HENRY: Nice fellow.

MELISSA: That word again.

(A beat. HENRY *looks around.)*

HENRY: You really live here.

MELISSA: Dad. What are you doing here?

HENRY: I have a meeting. In the Loop.

(HENRY *crosses to the table and pulls out the chair to sit. It wobbles dangerously.)*

(He pushes it back in and remains standing, looking around the place.)

MELISSA: You should've called.

HENRY: I didn't think you would take my call. And I really just wanted to talk…

MELISSA: To talk?

HENRY: Yes. *(Beat)* I should've called.

MELISSA: Yeah.

HENRY: I just needed to see you and I wanted to—

(The roar of the El train passing by shakes the whole apartment.)

(HENRY crosses to the window and watches the train as it goes by.)

HENRY: Jesus! That's…that's loud. How can you stand that?

MELISSA: I'm used to it.

HENRY: Our first apartment, your mother and I, was right beside the "L". It was a dump. *(Beat. He looks down at the street.)* There's my car. I parked it on the corner…in front of that boarded up building with all the graffiti—

MELISSA: Your car's fine, Dad.

HENRY: Is that a crack house?

MELISSA: Dad.

HENRY: You park on the street?

MELISSA: I don't have a car.

HENRY: Oh.

(MELISSA watches HENRY who can't remove his eyes from the street below.)

MELISSA: Dad, it's fine.

HENRY: I was just…I had to step over a bum to get into your building.

MELISSA: He's harmless. He just sleeps on the front steps sometimes.

HENRY: This neighborhood…

MELISSA: It's really up and coming.

HENRY: Up and coming. Huh.

MELISSA: You should've seen it two years ago.

HENRY walks around the apartment, looking around…
inspecting. It really is a great place to live. There are a
ton of little hole in the wall galleries and bars and it's
convenient. Not only am I a block from the blue line,
I'm only two doors down from my crack dealer.

(A beat)

HENRY: That's not funny.

*(MELISSA sips her coffee and watches HENRY as he inspects
her studio.)*

HENRY: It's cold in here. There's a draft. Is there a
window open or-

MELISSA: I should get ready for work.

*(MELISSA stands and crosses to her "bedroom" —behind the
room divider.)*

*(HENRY crosses to MELISSA's paintings and starts looking
at them.)*

MELISSA: Does Mom know you're here?

*(HENRY keeps looking through the paintings, avoiding her
question.)*

HENRY: Did you do all these paintings?

MELISSA: Yeah.

(HENRY looks at one in particular.)

*(MELISSA steps out from behind her room divider. Watches
him.)*

MELISSA: What do you think?

HENRY: This one is really…interesting.

MELISSA: Interesting.

HENRY: I don't know. You know I don't know anything about art. I just like it. Okay? It feels familiar.

MELISSA: That's because you've seen it before.

HENRY: Have I?

MELISSA: It's the one that got me into art school.

HENRY: Oh. Right. I thought I recognized it. *(He regards it some more)* How much? *(He pulls out his checkbook.)*

MELISSA: You want to buy it?

HENRY: A thousand?

MELISSA: A thousand dollars?!

HENRY: Fifteen hundred?

MELISSA: Dad—

HENRY: How much?

MELISSA: It's not worth more than a couple hundred.

HENRY: You're a terrible negotiator.

MELISSA: It's depressing, okay? My daddy buying one of my paintings because he feels sorry for me.

HENRY: You make your own choices. You are where you are by the choices you made.

MELISSA: Then, you're worried about me. I don't have a 401K, I—

(Another train passes. HENRY and MELISSA wait.)

MELISSA: I practically live on top of the El, I have a bum on my door step, I'm out of coffee—

HENRY: What does Jack think?

MELISSA: About what?

HENRY: About you living here. Doesn't he worry?

MELISSA: Jack knows I can take care of myself.

(HENRY looks at her then to his check book.)

HENRY: Fifteen hundred then.

MELISSA: You don't have to do this.

HENRY: I just want to buy the painting. I told you. I like it.

(HENRY hands MELISSA the check, but she doesn't take it.)

MELISSA: What did Mom say when you told her I came home for brunch?

HENRY: *(Beat)* I wanted to talk to you about that. She's been under a lot of...stress...lately.

MELISSA: Did she tell you she called me?

(Beat. HENRY just looks at MELISSA, trying to find the right approach.)

MELISSA: Dad? *(Beat)* I have a meeting with my boss. I can't be late. *(Beat)* HENRY: Do you want a ride? I can drop you off.

MELISSA: No.

HENRY: Melissa...

MELISSA: Thanks for the coffee, Dad.

(A beat)

HENRY: Well, I'll just... I'll just leave the check here. *(He places the check on the table.)*

MELISSA: Dad—

HENRY: Please. *(He picks up the painting and goes to the door.)*

(Just before exiting, HENRY turns back to MELISSA.)

HENRY: *(Regarding the painting)* I really do like it.

(HENRY exits. MELISSA looks at the check. Lights. End of scene)

Scene 6

(HENRY *and* CHARLOTTE's *living/dining room.*)

Lights up on CHARLOTTE staring at a blank space on the wall—where a Zen inspired painting used to hang (*And now sits on the floor.*)

(HENRY *enters carrying* MELISSA's *painting. He hangs it in the blank space. They both step back and take it in.*)

(CHARLOTTE *looks at* HENRY, *then the painting. He watches her reaction. She looks back at him.*)

CHARLOTTE: You really like this piece?

HENRY: You don't?

CHARLOTTE: Henry.

HENRY: What's wrong with it?

CHARLOTTE: It's… Not exactly my style.

HENRY: I like it.

CHARLOTTE: Where did you get it?

HENRY: Downtown.

CHARLOTTE: Where?

HENRY: Why does that matter?

CHARLOTTE: Because *you* don't buy art.

She steps closer to it and inspects it closely.

CHARLOTTE: Huh. It seems…it reminds me of something. I can't…I can't place it. It's clearly derivative, though. (*Beat*) You really like it?

HENRY: I do.

CHARLOTTE: It doesn't match anything in the house.

HENRY: Why does everything have to match?

CHARLOTTE: Hilary and I have worked really hard to create a peaceful environment in which to eat.

HENRY: Who's Hilary?

CHARLOTTE: Our interior decorator, Henry.

HENRY: I thought her name was Hannah.

CHARLOTTE: It's Hilary.

HENRY: I never liked that painting.

CHARLOTTE: Why didn't you say anything?

HENRY: I don't know.

CHARLOTTE: Well, it's integral in the design. Everything works together. Calming colors, ergonomic dining chairs, subtle lighting. It's all to create a tranquil dining experience and to aid the body with digestion.

HENRY: And this painting will upset that environment? One painting.

CHARLOTTE: It's hostile! Look at it. Those brush strokes are seething with anger. I don't want to look at that when I sit down to eat. I'll get indigestion. I'll have nightmares. I won't be able to sleep. I can't sleep as it is. Because I still can't find my Ambien and the stupid pharmacist wouldn't refill my prescription.

(HENRY *takes the painting down. He holds it protectively close to his chest.*)

HENRY: I'll just hang it in my office.

CHARLOTTE: Good idea. Win, win.

HENRY: *I* like it.

CHARLOTTE: Did you call her, Henry? About my pills?

HENRY: *(To himself)* It's not derivative.

(HENRY *crosses in the direction of his office.* CHARLOTTE *follows.*)

CHARLOTTE: I know she took them. She's probably selling them for money.

HENRY: She didn't take them, Charlotte.

CHARLOTTE: Who did, then?

(HENRY *stops and turns to face* CHARLOTTE.)

HENRY: No one took your Ambien, Charlotte.

CHARLOTTE: So they just evaporated?

HENRY: You finished them.

CHARLOTTE: *I* did.

HENRY: Yes.

CHARLOTTE: Oh, okay.

HENRY: Charlotte, you haven't needed sleeping pills for almost a year. That's why the pharmacist wouldn't refill your prescription. Because you haven't had one for *almost a year.*

(A long beat)

CHARLOTTE: *(Convinced) You* took them.

(CHARLOTTE *takes a step back.* HENRY *reaches out and puts his hand gently on her shoulder.*)

HENRY: Charlotte.

CHARLOTTE: Don't touch me.

(CHARLOTTE *shrugs* HENRY *off and backs away.*)

CHARLOTTE: I'm calling my doctor.

(HENRY *reaches for* CHARLOTTE *again.*)

HENRY: Charlotte.

CHARLOTTE: I said don't touch me!

(CHARLOTTE *exits. A beat as* HENRY *watches her go. He looks at the painting in his hands and exits, carrying it off.*)

Scene 7

(JACK *and* MELISSA *at* MELISSA's *place.* JACK *is fixing the chair while* MELISSA *sips grappa.*)

MELISSA: You don't have to do that.

JACK: I want to.

MELISSA: You're always helping me.

JACK: Because I want to.

MELISSA: I'm fine.

JACK: Okay.

MELISSA: I'm supposed to be making you dinner.

JACK: We can order pizza or something.

MELISSA: I just want to make it up to you. How I behaved the other day.

JACK: You already apologized. It's fine.

MELISSA: I'm so embarrassed. You were right. I put you in an incredibly awkward position—

JACK: It's fine.

MELISSA: I turned right back into a child just being in that house.

JACK: We could order Italian. My treat.

MELISSA: Jack.

JACK: It's no big deal. I've got money.

(MELISSA *holds up the check.*)

MELISSA: I do too. Fifteen hundred big ones from Dad—

JACK: You need that for rent.

(*Beat.* MELISSA *sips the grappa. Grimaces*)

MELISSA: I'd rather not need anything. I don't want to be needy.

JACK: You were just fired.

MELISSA: Laid off.

JACK: Let me treat.

MELISSA: No one buys books anymore.

JACK: Pizza or pasta?

MELISSA: I don't want to live in a society where no one buys books.

JACK: Do you have a menu?

He searches for a menu.

MELISSA: I should move.

JACK: I'm in the mood for lasagna.

(MELISSA *takes another sip. Grimaces*)

MELISSA: This is awful.

JACK: It's an acquired taste.

MELISSA: Grappa?

JACK: It's eighty proof. You should really eat something. Let's order.

MELISSA: Italian. Sounds good. Maybe I'll move to Italy. People buy books in Italy. And they appreciate art. And American women. *(Beat)* Tastes like paint thinner.

JACK: It's made by distilling the leavings of—

MELISSA: The leavings?

JACK: The leftovers. What's left of the grapes at bottom of the barrel after making wine. They call it pomace. It's comprised of the skins of grapes and their seeds. The leavings.

MELISSA: No wonder it tastes so yummy.

JACK: It's actually a perfect example of recycling ingenuity.

(MELISSA *laughs.*)

JACK: What? It is. Nothing wasted.

MELISSA: I love that about you.

JACK: You do?

MELISSA: You're so nerdy.

JACK: Oh.

MELISSA: It's cute. *(She gulps the grappa.)*

JACK: Careful. It's meant to be sipped. Not guzzled.

MELISSA: I'm fine. I'll be fine.

JACK: Will you?

MELISSA: Yes.

JACK: What are you gonna do?

MELISSA: Finish this drink then order some food.

JACK: And then?

MELISSA: Eat the food. Cash my dad's check. Buy a
one-way ticket to Romania and find a job as a traveling
magician's assistant.

(Beat)

JACK: I just want you to be happy.

MELISSA: Like my dad?

JACK: No. Not like your dad. *(Beat. He changes. He is
suddenly all man.)* Not at all. *(He leans in and kisses her.)*

(But MELISSA doesn't kiss back.)

(JACK pulls away.)

(MELISSA just looks straight ahead.)

(Mortified)

JACK: Oh. Fuck. So, that's it?

MELISSA: What?

JACK: What do you mean, what? I just—and you just—
(Beat) Fuck!

MELISSA: I did not know you were gonna do that.

JACK: That's incredibly insulting.

MELISSA: Insulting? You just, out of the blue—

JACK: Out of the blue?! Are you fucking kidding me?

MELISSA: I had no idea you even felt like that.

JACK: Of course.

MELISSA: I thought you were my friend.

JACK: Your friend?!

MELISSA: My friend. Yes.

JACK: Your friend. Yeah. I am your friend.

MELISSA: Then you could see how weirded-out I might
be by your sudden change of attitude towards me.
Right?

JACK: Right. Sure.

MELISSA: I mean, I just got laid-off. I'm drunk. I'm
fucked. And…then you suddenly change…like that.
Like you want something from me. Like I'm suddenly
some piece of…ass!

JACK: Oh, just…please just stop.

MELISSA: I didn't know…I had no idea you wanted
anything like that from me.

JACK: I don't.

MELISSA: You don't?

JACK: No.

(A beat)

MELISSA: Then what was that?

JACK: A moment. Just…a moment. *(Beat)* Forget it. It's
already gone. *(He goes for his coat.)*

MELISSA: You're leaving? What about dinner?

(JACK *opens the door.*)

MELISSA: Jack!

(JACK *exits, slamming the door behind him. End of scene*)

Scene 8

(HENRY *and* CHARLOTTE's *family room.*)

(*Lights up on* CHARLOTTE *decorating a Christmas tree. Christmas music plays in the background.*)

(CHARLOTTE *hangs an ornament on the tree, then crosses to the table where she pours herself an extra large glass of wine.*)

(HENRY *enters. As soon as he hears the music and sees* CHARLOTTE, *he stops and just watches, in awe.*)

(CHARLOTTE *turns and sees him.*)

CHARLOTTE: Oh, honey, you're home. I didn't hear you come in. I had a hell of a day!

(CHARLOTTE *takes a big sip of wine.* HENRY *watches.*)

HENRY: You…you got the tree out.

CHARLOTTE: I needed to distract myself from my awful day. Thought a little decorating might cheer me up. Get me in the spirit, you know? (*Beat*) Henry. Take your coat off. Stay a while.

(HENRY *just stands there.* CHARLOTTE *takes his coat off for him, singing along to the music.*)

CHARLOTTE: Come on. Let's sit. (*She sits on the couch with her glass of wine, knees tucked up under herself, and pats the couch next to her.*) Sit with me.

(HENRY *complies.*)

CHARLOTTE: You're brooding. It's sexy. You're always handsome. But especially when you brood. It makes me want to crawl inside of you.

HENRY: Charlotte—

CHARLOTTE: I can't help it. I married a handsome and sexy man.

HENRY: Can we turn the music off?

CHARLOTTE: I have something to tell you. And you'll never believe it. You will never believe it. Are you ready? Today for the first time in my entire life, I was fired. Well, "laid off". Walter is selling the company. And he needs, his words, "to trim the fat." I'm the fat, I guess. After ten years. You believe that? Ten years of finding other people jobs I'm now the one who needs a headhunter. I need me. But I can't help me. I don't want find myself a job.

HENRY: Charlotte.

CHARLOTTE: It doesn't feel good, Henry. Being fired. Walter. Screw him. He's a pompous ass, anyway. (*She takes a huge sip of wine.*)

HENRY: Easy.

CHARLOTTE: And as if losing my job wasn't enough, I got a speeding ticket for going fifty-three in a forty-five zone. Which was just perfect because I was on my way to pick up Melissa—. Where is she? Is she with you?

(HENRY *stands and crosses to the stereo.*)

CHARLOTTE: What are you doing?

HENRY: Don't you think it's a little early for Christmas music, Charlotte?

CHARLOTTE: It's never too early to get in the spirit.

HENRY: But…it's May. Charlotte. It's May.
You're decorating for Christmas and it's only May.

(A beat. CHARLOTTE *just looks at* HENRY *and starts laughing.)*

*(*HENRY *takes the wine out of her hand and sets it down on a nearby table.)*

CHARLOTTE: What are you doing?!

*(*CHARLOTTE *reaches for the wine and* HENRY *holds her back.)*

HENRY: We need to talk, Charlotte.

CHARLOTTE: I've got laundry.

HENRY: Walter sold the company five years ago.

CHARLOTTE: I don't need this. Not today.

HENRY: You didn't get fired today. You haven't worked in five years.

CHARLOTTE: I know that.

HENRY: You called our daughter and invited her to brunch and then totally forgot about it—

CHARLOTTE: Not this again!

HENRY: You got lost on the way home from Jewel—

CHARLOTTE: I told you I tried a short cut.

HENRY: You lose your way in conversation—

CHARLOTTE: I've been tired!

HENRY: You forgot our anniversary—

CHARLOTTE: You always forget our anniversary!

HENRY: Appointments, people's names, dinner plans—

CHARLOTTE: I'm tired of being the one to always have to remember everything!!

HENRY: Charlotte—

CHARLOTTE: Maybe I don't want to be in charge anymore, Henry. Ever think of that?!

HENRY: You aren't yourself!

CHARLOTTE: Stop.

HENRY: You aren't yourself, Charlotte.

CHARLOTTE: *(Begging)* Henry, please.

HENRY: It's May 3rd. And you're decorating for Christmas as if it were November.

(Beat. No response from CHARLOTTE.*)*

HENRY: Maybe you're scared. But…

CHARLOTTE: I'm going for a walk.

HENRY: Charlotte.

CHARLOTTE: Dinner's in the oven. *(Sarcastic)* Somehow I managed to remember that.

*(*CHARLOTTE *exits.* HENRY *lets her go.)*

*(*HENRY *stands for a beat. Then he sits. He leans forward as if waiting for something to happen. He leans back and loosens his tie. He breathes. A beat)*

(The smoke alarm goes off from the kitchen. HENRY *sits up.)*

HENRY: Charlotte?!

*(*HENRY's *up. He's exiting towards the kitchen. Lights shift, suggesting a passage of time.)*

Scene 9

(Later that night. A phone rings on stage—the sound is muffled. HENRY *enters with a phone to his ear, he searches for the source of the ringing.)*

(He finds CHARLOTTE's *purse under a blanket and pulls her ringing cell phone out.)*

(He hangs up. He opens her phone and scrolls through the numbers. He finds one and dials.)

HENRY: *(Into phone)* No, Sheila, it's— … Hi… Fine. No, that's actually why I'm calling. I thought she might be with you…

(CHARLOTTE *enters downstage right and crosses to downstage left. She's soaked from head to toe and holds herself tightly. She takes a few moments, looking around, disconnected.)*

(CHARLOTTE *slowly sits. She shivers.)*

HENRY: *(Into phone)* We just…she was a little…upset and…I just thought she might have walked over to your place…

CHARLOTTE: This doesn't feel like it should.

HENRY: *(Into phone)* Well, it's been a few hours. She should have been back by now.

CHARLOTTE: It's colder than I remember.

(There's a light suddenly shining in her face. She shields her eyes. A SECURITY GUARD *[played by the same actor as* MELISSA*] enters, shining a flashlight at* CHARLOTTE.*)*

SECURITY GUARD: Hello? Is someone there?

CHARLOTTE: Finally.

SECURITY GUARD: Ma'am?

CHARLOTTE: I've been waiting.

SECURITY GUARD: This is private property.

CHARLOTTE: Could you please not shine that directly into my eyes?

SECURITY GUARD: Can I help you with something?

CHARLOTTE: Melissa, if you don't turn that flashlight off by the count of three, I *will* take it away from you. *(She finally looks at the* SECURITY GUARD. *A beat)* One!

SECURITY GUARD: You're soaking wet.

CHARLOTTE: Two!

SECURITY GUARD: You okay?

CHARLOTTE: Three!

(The SECURITY GUARD *turns the flashlight off.)*

CHARLOTTE: *(To* SECURITY GUARD*)* Thank you.

HENRY: *(Into phone)* If you could just come here and wait for her in case she comes back. That way I can go out and look— No. I understand.

SECURITY GUARD: You called me Melissa. Who's Melissa?

CHARLOTTE: I know what you did.

HENRY: —

CHARLOTTE: You stole my pills again, didn't you?

SECURITY GUARD: Can you stand for me, Ma'am?

CHARLOTTE: I just want them back. So that I can sleep.

CHARLOTTE's phone rings.

HENRY: *(Into phone)* Hello? No, Sheila. She left it. Yes. Right.

CHARLOTTE: I won't tell anyone. If you just return them, we can pretend this never happened.

HENRY: *(Into phone)* You'll call me if she turns up. Okay? Thank you.

SECURITY GUARD: Ma'am—

HENRY: *(Into phone)* Good night, Sheila. *(Pause)* No, I just… Sitting and waiting is not an option.

SECURITY GUARD: You keep calling me Melissa. Who's Melissa?

CHARLOTTE: Very funny.

SECURITY GUARD: You're not okay, are you?

CHARLOTTE: I'm fine.

HENRY: *(Into phone)* Okay, fine.

SECURITY GUARD: You don't seem fine.

CHARLOTTE: I'm fine.

HENRY: *(Into phone)* Sure.

CHARLOTTE: Fine.

(SECURITY GUARD offers her coat to CHARLOTTE. She places it around her shoulders.)

SECURITY GUARD: Ma'am—

CHARLOTTE: Stop calling me ma'am!

SECURITY GUARD: What's your name?

(CHARLOTTE looks at the SECURITY GUARD for a long beat. A realization dawns.)

CHARLOTTE: Charlotte. Scott.

SECURITY GUARD: Gina Kelly.

(CHARLOTTE and SECURITY GUARD shake.)

CHARLOTTE: Nice to meet you.

HENRY: *(Into phone)* A drink? I don't need a drink. I need my wife.

SECURITY GUARD: So, Ms Scott—

CHARLOTTE: Mrs.

SECURITY GUARD: Mrs. Were you in that water? Do you know how cold that water is?

CHARLOTTE: Colder than I remember.

SECURITY GUARD: Did you fall—?

HENRY: *(Into phone)* Waxing? I'm just calling numbers in my wife's phone.
What is a waxing salon?

SECURITY GUARD: Are you hurt?

HENRY: *(Into phone)* Sorry to bother you.

SECURITY GUARD: I think maybe I should get you to the hospital.

CHARLOTTE: No!

HENRY: *(To himself)* Maybe I'm overreacting. *(Into phone)* I'm, I'm wondering if you might have a Charlotte Scott there...Charlotte. Scott. Yes, I'll hold.

SECURITY GUARD: You could be in shock or something.

CHARLOTTE: I'm fine.

SECURITY GUARD: That water is pretty cold. 40 degrees.

CHARLOTTE: I said I'm fine.

SECURITY GUARD: That's cold.

CHARLOTTE: I'm/

SECURITY GUARD: Mrs. Scott

CHARLOTTE: Fine.

SECURITY GUARD: You really don't seem fine.

CHARLOTTE: I just went for a swim.

SECURITY GUARD: In Lake Michigan. In May. At night. By yourself?

CHARLOTTE: Look. I'd really like to just sit here. Alone. Okay?

SECURITY GUARD: I'm sorry. But that's just not possible. I can give you a ride home. Where do you live?

(No response)

SECURITY GUARD: Is there a mister we could call?

CHARLOTTE: *(As if remembering)* Henry.

SECURITY GUARD: Let's call him.

(CHARLOTTE pulls out her cell phone.)

SECURITY GUARD: What's his number?

CHARLOTTE: I'm sorry to trouble you. *(She gets up.)*

SECURITY GUARD: It's no trouble. You wanna call?

(SECURITY GUARD holds the phone out to CHARLOTTE. CHARLOTTE looks at the phone. She takes it. And stares at the numbers.)

SECURITY GUARD: It's okay. It won't bite.

(CHARLOTTE hands the phone back.)

CHARLOTTE: I think I'll just walk.

SECURITY GUARD: I'll give you a lift home.

CHARLOTTE: No. It's not far. I can walk.

SECURITY GUARD: You're soaking wet.

CHARLOTTE: I'm sorry to have troubled you. Thank you for your help. *(She walks off.)*

SECURITY GUARD: Mrs Scott. *(Beat)* Wait! *(She follows.)*

HENRY: Yes, I'm still here. She's not. Well, I appreciate your checking. *(Beat)* You as well. *(He snaps the phone shut.)*

(HENRY calls CHARLOTTE's phone. It rings.)

HENRY: *(Into phone)* Char? It's me. I'm here. At home. And you're out there...somewhere. Without your phone or purse or car or coat and... *(Long beat)* I'm sorry.

(JACK enters answering his phone.)

JACK: Hi. Hello.

(MELISSA enters in her pajamas, brushing her teeth and talking on the phone.)

MELISSA: I didn't hear my phone.

JACK: What?

MELISSA: When you called.

JACK: Oh, that's okay.

(HENRY *looks at* CHARLOTTE'*s phone in his hand. He picks up his cell phone and scrolls through the numbers.*)

JACK: I just wanted to see if we could talk—

MELISSA: *(With toothbrush in mouth)* Come over.

JACK: What?

(MELISSA *removes the toothbrush.*)

MELISSA: Sorry. Toothbrush. Why don't you come over?

JACK: Now?

MELISSA: Why not?

JACK: Melissa...

MELISSA: Is this about the...awkward moment we're pretending didn't happen but did?

JACK: No, it's not.

MELISSA: I just don't want things to be weird between us.

JACK: It's about a conversation I had with my father today.

MELISSA: About the mayor's wife?

JACK: What?

MELISSA: The commission. Remember? You said your father knew—

JACK: No. No, this isn't about that.

MELISSA: Oh.

JACK: I spoke with my father today. And...I don't know how to say this, but...he...made a decision.

(HENRY *dials and puts the phone to his ear.*)

MELISSA: Ooh. Can you hold on? I've got another call.

JACK: No. I can't hold.

MELISSA: Okay, but just—

JACK: Do not put me on hold!

HENRY: *(Into phone)* Melissa, it's Dad. Call me back. Please. It's an emergency. *(He hangs up.)*

MELISSA: What's going on, Jack?

JACK: It's about the show.

MELISSA: What about it?

JACK: It's been…cancelled.

MELISSA: What?

JACK: Postponed…indefinitely.

MELISSA: Why?!

JACK: Well, my father doesn't feel your work is ready and with this economy it's a better move for us to go with someone more…

MELISSA: More what?

JACK: More…established.

(No response)

JACK: Hello?

MELISSA: You're telling me this on the phone.

JACK: I didn't think you'd want to see me in person after…I just thought this would be…easier.

MELISSA: For you.

JACK: *(Beat)* It's not personal.

MELISSA: You said you had faith in me. You said.

JACK: We believe…I've always believed…hoped. I'm sorry. I really am. *(He picks up his painting, looks at it, and exits.)*

(CHARLOTTE wanders back on stage. She looks completely lost. She looks around, then finds a spot and sits.)

MELISSA: Jack? *(She looks at her phone. She lowers it. She drags the toothbrush across her teeth in a complete daze.)*

*(*HENRY *tries again.* MELISSA*'s phone rings. She answers.)*

MELISSA: Hello?

HENRY: Melissa, thank God.

MELISSA: Daddy?

HENRY: I need your help. It's your Mom. I need you to help me find her.

(End of Scene)

END OF ACT ONE

ACT TWO

Scene 1

(CHARLOTTE and HENRY'S)

(The middle of the night)

(MELISSA is asleep on the couch.)

(The living room is illuminated by the moonlight.)

(CHARLOTTE enters in a nightgown. She glides like a ghost to the center of the room where she stands looking out for a beat.)

(She looks around…)

(Crosses to the Christmas tree and begins to take the ornaments off the tree and replace them in the box.)

(She drops a glass bulb. It shatters. Wakes MELISSA. She bolts upright startling CHARLOTTE.)

MELISSA: Mom?

CHARLOTTE: Damn it.

MELISSA: What time is it?

CHARLOTTE: I dropped a bulb.

MELISSA: Are you…are you okay?

CHARLOTTE: It was one of my favorites. The hand-painted one from Saint Lucia. I loved that bulb. Remember that trip? Remember how Santa arrived in a kayak?

MELISSA: I didn't mean to fall asleep. Is Dad here?

CHARLOTTE: *(In a sing song, not how Santa usually says it)* Ho ho ho HO ho ho. *(Beat)* Remember that? Ho ho ho HO ho ho. *(Beat)* You don't remember?

MELISSA: No. I remember. Ho ho ho HO ho ho.

CHARLOTTE: So funny. You didn't like it. You wanted snow, Santa in a sleigh not a kayak and just three hos. *(Looks at the broken ornament)* Now it's broken.

(A beat)

MELISSA: Dad was looking for you. He was worried.

CHARLOTTE: He always worries. He was born worrying.

MELISSA: You seem...

CHARLOTTE: Did you finish your Algebra homework?

(No response)

CHARLOTTE: You're teetering on a B in that class. It requires an extra effort. I know you think it's not a big deal, but your freshman year in high school sets the tone for your entire high school experience—

MELISSA: High school?

CHARLOTTE: Trust me. You don't want a B on your record. You don't want to have to come back from that. Besides the fact that you're better than a B. You are. You're my smart little angel. My little smarty pants.

MELISSA: Mom—

CHARLOTTE: There's no reason you shouldn't get straight A's. If you pay attention in class and don't let your mind wander—

MELISSA: Mom! *(A beat)* Are you...sleep walking??

CHARLOTTE: Why is it that whenever grades come up you always try to change the subject?

MELISSA: Hi. I'm Melissa. Your daughter you haven't seen in two years. *(Beat)* It's good to see you too.

(A moment)

CHARLOTTE: That's a new couch. *(A slight beat)* An expensive couch. It's not for sleeping.

MELISSA: Dad said you disappeared. He was really worried.

CHARLOTTE: Must be nice to sleep like that. Without the help of sleeping pills.

MELISSA: Why is the tree out?

(A long beat)

CHARLOTTE: I don't want you sleeping on this couch.

MELISSA: It's actually really comfortable.

CHARLOTTE: We just put a new bed in the guest room.

MELISSA: Mom, why are you decorating the Christmas tree?

CHARLOTTE: So you've decided to grace us with your presence. To what do we owe the honor?

MELISSA: Dad asked for my help—

CHARLOTTE: And you agreed? Why? *(Beat)* The truth.

MELISSA: *(After a beat)* You sounded kind.

CHARLOTTE: I sounded kind?

MELISSA: In your message. When you called to invite me to brunch.

CHARLOTTE: Oh, sweetie. I never called you and you know it. I don't know what sort of angle you're playing here, but—

MELISSA: You did. You called me.

CHARLOTTE: Okay.

MELISSA: You did.

CHARLOTTE: You might just try coming out and saying, "Mom, I miss you. And I'm sorry. I apologize." It's not hard. Try it. "I apologize."

MELISSA: For what?

CHARLOTTE: For what. For stealing my pills. For lying to my face. For disrespecting your father. For abandoning us—

MELISSA: Come on—

CHARLOTTE: You did. You abandoned us.

MELISSA: You're being dramatic.

CHARLOTTE: You just walked away one day. Moved away—

MELISSA: To the city. To Chicago. Not Mogadishu.

CHARLOTTE: No word. No visits. No phone calls. You made it very clear you didn't want us around. Didn't want me around. Didn't want—

MELISSA: I couldn't take it anymore!

(No response)

MELISSA: You pushed me. All. The. Time. Pushing me, nagging, manipulating. Nothing I did was ever good enough for you. I wanted to go to art school, you—

CHARLOTTE: You turned down a scholarship to Northwestern!

(MELISSA stops. Then;)

MELISSA: Nine years ago. Nine years ago I turned down a scholarship to Northwestern. Yes.

CHARLOTTE: With no thought to your parents, your future—

MELISSA: Yep. I'm just a total fuck up and we're never gonna get past this, are we?

(A beat. Then CHARLOTTE *spots* MELISSA's *purse, crosses to it and digs through the contents.)*

MELISSA: What are you doing?

CHARLOTTE: I know you have them. You took them.

MELISSA: What?

CHARLOTTE: My Ambien!

*(*MELISSA *looks at* CHARLOTTE—*totally perplexed. A beat. Then;)*

MELISSA: *(Calling off)* Dad?!

CHARLOTTE: Your father believes me. He won't help you out of this.

MELISSA: Dad!!!

*(*CHARLOTTE *dumps the contents out and rifles through the spilled contents on the floor.)*

CHARLOTTE: What have you done with them? Just tell me! I know you have them!

*(*HENRY *appears.)*

HENRY: Charlotte?

*(*CHARLOTTE *just looks at* HENRY.*)*

(She stands.)

CHARLOTTE: I know she took them. They might not be here in her purse. But she took them, Henry. *(She exits.)*

(A long moment)

HENRY: She's…

MELISSA: Insane?

HENRY: She doesn't sleep at night anymore. She gets up. Tries to… *(He shakes his head.)*

MELISSA: She's taking pills again. You didn't tell me that. One minute she's taking down the Christmas

tree talking about Saint Lucia, the next she's digging
through my shit like a fucking junkie!

(Off HENRY's look:)

MELISSA: I'm not lying. Jesus, nobody believes me in
this house.

HENRY: I believe you.

MELISSA: You do. So Mom's a junkie?

HENRY: Your mother is not a junkie.

MELISSA: Okay.

HENRY: Okay. Your mother. She gets up in the middle
of the night to, uh, start her day. The other night
she got up at two-twenty-seven and called Judy to
schedule a coffee date. Blamed it on sleep walking.
In the thirty years I've been sharing a bed with your
mother she's never once walked in her sleep. Tonight
I found her window shopping at Plaza del Lago. Her
hair was wet. Clothes soaked through. Head to toe.

MELISSA: Dad—

HENRY: I didn't want to see it. Let myself believe it
was nothing. But it's not nothing anymore. Not after
tonight. This is how it started.

MELISSA: How what started?

HENRY: Your grandmother.

(MELISSA processes this.)

MELISSA: Mom's young.

HENRY: I know. I God damn know.

MELISSA: She's too young.

HENRY: She tries so hard to cover. I watch her. I see her
process. Searching for the right word, right response…
Last week I saw her get confused about how to make
the bed. It was like she suddenly forgot how and when

she saw me watching her she just threw the blanket
down and said she's tired of making the bed every day
and if I wanted it made I could do it myself.

MELISSA: Well, she has a point.

HENRY: She's good at covering. And the whole brunch
thing with you...

MELISSA: Oh.

HENRY: I knew then.

(Long beat. Then:)

HENRY: Uh, you could stay in your old room. It has a
new bed now. It's really comfortable. It's...a queen.
You have a full, right? Queen's bigger. Better sleep.

MELISSA: Dad—

HENRY: You could set up a studio. In the garage.

MELISSA: What?

HENRY: Or the shed. Or right here. Put your easel by
the picture window if you want. Whatever you want.
We'll figure it out.

MELISSA: You want me to move back in?

HENRY: What I know is that I can't do this alone.

MELISSA: For how long?

HENRY: I don't know. I'll pay you.

MELISSA: What would I do?

HENRY: You'd live here. You'd be available to help.
To...

MELISSA: Baby sit.

HENRY: I need someone with her while I'm at work.

MELISSA: She's not gonna like that.

HENRY: We'll figure it out.

MELISSA: She won't like it at all.

HENRY: None of us likes it. But it can't be ignored anymore.

MELISSA: This could be...more than I can...I mean, I want to help. But...and she won't want me in her way.. Taking care...she won't.

HENRY: Just a few weeks. While we figure things out. Could you do that? A few weeks? Do you think you could work that out with your job? Maybe take a temporary leave or something? I'll pay you.

MELISSA: My job won't be a problem. I just—

HENRY: I'll pay you. I said. I will. Just a few weeks. While we figure things out. We can do that, right? Meli-bean?

(End of scene)

Scene 2

(CHARLOTTE sits on the couch reading.)

(She looks up as HENRY enters carrying an easel and a box of paints.)

CHARLOTTE: What do you have there? What is that?

HENRY: Oh. It's an easel.

(MELISSA enters carrying a large duffel bag.)

MELISSA: Hello. Mom. Dad, I'm just gonna... *(She nods towards the stairs)*

HENRY: Sure. You go on up.

MELISSA exits up the stairs.

(Answering CHARLOTTE's look:)

HENRY: It's just for a little while.

CHARLOTTE: What is?

HENRY: Now, don't get excited.

CHARLOTTE: Don't get excited? What?

HENRY: Well, we decided…I asked her…because I thought…

CHARLOTTE: Would you just say it. Have the nerve to do that. Say it.

HENRY: You're getting worked up.

CHARLOTTE: I'm not getting worked up. I'm perfectly calm. I just want to know why things are happening around me in my house without my knowledge. And my own husband won't just come out and tell me.

HENRY: Melissa's going to be staying with us for a while. *(Beat)* If that's…okay…

CHARLOTTE: If that's okay.

HENRY: No. She's staying. Either way.

CHARLOTTE: Unbelievable.

HENRY: I thought you'd be happy. It was…it's for you.

CHARLOTTE: You didn't even ask me.

HENRY: It's a good thing. We're all together. Don't you want our daughter here?

CHARLOTTE: What kind of a mother would I be if I didn't want my own daughter in my home?

HENRY: So she can stay?

CHARLOTTE: No!

HENRY sets the easel down.

CHARLOTTE: Not without a discussion. Not without consulting me. Talking to me. Hello! I'm here! I live here too!

(Beat)

HENRY: I should have talked to you first.

CHARLOTTE: This is my house too.

HENRY: It's only for a little while. I just need some help with things.

CHARLOTTE: I help you. You don't need somebody else.

HENRY: I do, Charlotte. That's what I keep telling you but you won't listen. You don't want to hear it. I tell you the same things over and over and you forget and it's been going on for too long and things are getting worse and I'm tired of being the only one who knows it. Who deals with it.

(A very long beat)

CHARLOTTE: It. *I'm* the "it."

(No response)

CHARLOTTE: No paints in the house. She can use the shed.

HENRY: Thank you.

CHARLOTTE just looks at him and exits towards the kitchen. HENRY exits towards the shed with the easel.

Scene 3

(PET scan)

(An image of CHARLOTTE's *brain. It looks like irregular splotches of orange red and green on a black background.)*

*(*CHARLOTTE *and* HENRY *sit with the* DOCTOR *[played by the same actor who plays* JACK*] looking up at the image.)*

(The DOCTOR *talks and points w/ a laser pointer to the image.)*

DOCTOR: Positron emission tomography. The PET scan holds crucial information regarding the level of chemical activity in the brain. The Hippocampus—

HENRY: Hippocampus?

DOCTOR: The part of the brain associated with learning and memory. This is what interests us. Here.

HENRY: Okay.

DOCTOR: See, we highlight glucose consumption patterns within the Hippocampus which will help us properly diagnose.

HENRY: Uh huh.

DOCTOR: Accurate diagnosis is imperative for proper treatment.

HENRY: Of course.

DOCTOR: We need to answer the "what" before we can address the "how".

(CHARLOTTE *sits up.*)

CHARLOTTE: We already know the "who".

HENRY: We didn't do this for Charlotte's mother.

DOCTOR: Well, it's new technology.

HENRY: She was misdiagnosed for years.

DOCTOR: That can happen.

HENRY: They thought she was just depressed and sent her to a psychiatrist who sent her back to the doctors with a note that there was nothing psychologically wrong with this woman.

DOCTOR: A note?

HENRY: She knew it was neurological. So did we. The doctors didn't. Why is that?

DOCTOR: We tend to want to see what we're dealing with and when we can't see it...

CHARLOTTE: I've never wondered who I am. I've always known.

HENRY: Right.

DOCTOR: But now we have this.

HENRY: Positron emission tomography.

DOCTOR: PET.

CHARLOTTE: PET. Irregular spots of rainbow colors on a black background.

DOCTOR: You can see from the scan—here—that the blood flow to the right side of the brain is significantly reduced. See? Here.

HENRY: Ah. Yes.

CHARLOTTE: I've always known who I am. To my bones.

DOCTOR: These spots here. And here. See how they're dark? Everything can be explained in those black spots—

HENRY: Everything?

DOCTOR: The gaps in time, the memory lapses—

CHARLOTTE: The skips and loops in my mind—

DOCTOR: The change in temperament.

CHARLOTTE: The skips and loops in my mind.

DOCTOR: The wandering, forgetting, losing—

CHARLOTTE: Train of thought. Derailed.

DOCTOR: It's all here.

CHARLOTTE: Skips and loops in my mind. Circling back. And back.

DOCTOR: And we know from the pattern that it isn't anything else.

HENRY: The pattern?

DOCTOR: It's distinct. And that's how we know what it is.

HENRY stares at the scan. At the black spots. The pattern. A beat.

DOCTOR: I know it's not...but isn't it better to know? To have an explanation. The critical information. We can now begin the fight. Armed. Ready for battle.

CHARLOTTE: I've never wondered who I am. I've always known. Now... I wonder all the time. I wonder who I am. I wonder *where* I am. How I got here. Where I'm going. Why I can't remember little things. Why I don't want to be around people. Get out of bed. Look in the mirror. Or recognize myself when I do. *(Beat)* I am losing power over myself. I trace the walls like a blind woman searching for something familiar. The way back home. And when I do find that thread of familiarity it leads me further back to the past each time. All of this I can see. All of this I understand. Just like I understand that the day will come when I wake up and all the questions will be gone. And so will I. And when that day comes, it will be a relief. But I'm not there yet.

(She gets off the table and crosses to HENRY *and* DOCTOR.)
(She looks up at her brain scan.)

DOCTOR: Those black spots explain everything.

CHARLOTTE: They don't explain everything. They don't explain how I feel. They don't show how it feels.

DOCTOR: No. I suppose not. But that's not really what I meant. I meant—

CHARLOTTE: I know what you meant.

DOCTOR: Okay. *(Beat)* Good. *(He takes out a prescription pad.)*
(Writes the prescriptions.)

DOCTOR: Studies show... People, patients of mine have reported a reversal of certain symptoms thanks to the combined effort of these medications.

HENRY: Reversal?

DOCTOR: Yes. Not just a slowing. But an actual reversal.

HENRY: That's great. Isn't that, Charlotte? It's something at least.

DOCTOR: We can keep you in Preserved Insight, treading water so to speak, for as long as possible.

CHARLOTTE: Sounds delightful.

HENRY: Preserved insight?

DOCTOR: Ah, it's what we call the early period. Before the patient becomes unaware of their situation.

CHARLOTTE: Blissfully unaware?

DOCTOR: Well…that's not what you want. You're not present then. You want to be present. Aware.

CHARLOTTE: My mother told me that she wished she had killed herself before she was erased from the inside out. That's what she said. Erased. From the inside out.

HENRY: Char…

CHARLOTTE: I wish I didn't know.

DOCTOR: Things are very different now than when your mother went through this. The medications are better, the awareness is better… you should join a group. A support group. People your age going through the same thing. You're not alone. You'd be surprised.

HENRY: A support group couldn't hurt.

(HENRY *and* DOCTOR *look to* CHARLOTTE *for a response.*)

CHARLOTTE: I just wish I didn't know what's coming next.

(*Lights. End of scene*)

Scene 4

(HENRY *and* MELISSA *sit at the kitchen table while* CHARLOTTE *serves dinner. Campbell's tomato soup from the can.*)

(HENRY *tries it.*)

HENRY: Mmm. This is the best soup I've ever had. Thank you, Charlotte.

CHARLOTTE: It's Campbell's from the can, honey.

HENRY: Well, it's delicious. Thank you for such a wonderful dinner.

CHARLOTTE: Don't thank me. All I did was open the can.

(MELISSA *tries it. Makes a face*)

CHARLOTTE: What?

MELISSA: *(Yuck)* Mmmmmm....

(CHARLOTTE *tastes it herself. Spits it out*)

CHARLOTTE: It's cold. It's cold, Henry. You said it was the best soup you've ever had and it's ice cold.

HENRY: Isn't it supposed to be? I thought it was gazpacho.

CHARLOTTE: When have I ever made gazpacho?

HENRY: I was just trying to be suppor—

CHARLOTTE: More like insulting. Condescending. Give me a break. *(She takes his soup away.)*

HENRY: I'm sorry. Here. I'll warm it up.

(HENRY *takes the soup from* CHARLOTTE *and* MELISSA *and goes to the stove to warm it up.* CHARLOTTE *sits, arms folded across her chest.*)

(MELISSA *watches her.*)

(CHARLOTTE *laughs a little to herself.*)

CHARLOTTE: *(Imitating* HENRY*)* This is the best soup I've ever had! Yum. Mmmmm.

*(*CHARLOTTE *laughs.* MELISSA *laughs too.* CHARLOTTE *gives her a look.* MELISSA *stops.)*

MELISSA: Sorry.

CHARLOTTE: No. Thank you for laughing. It's funny. It is. I drove home today. Without the G P S. Made every turn. But soup. That's tricky.

HENRY: The medicine will help. Once you give it a chance to work—

CHARLOTTE: They'll love this story in group.

HENRY: Are you liking group better?

CHARLOTTE: I don't think it's something you're supposed to like.

HENRY: I just mean—

CHARLOTTE: Are *you* liking group, Henry?

*(*HENRY *doesn't respond.)*

MELISSA: You're going to a support group, Dad?

CHARLOTTE: Yes, he is. He didn't think I'd find out. But I still have my ways.

MELISSA: Oh, I don't doubt it.

(A beat)

HENRY: *(Changing the subject)* So, Meli, how's your commission coming along?

MELISSA: Oh. Fine. Yeah.

HENRY: You've been spending a lot of time in your studio. Must be coming along.

CHARLOTTE: Her studio? It's a shed. A tool shed.

HENRY: Not anymore. Now it's a studio. *(To* MELISSA*)* How's it coming?

MELISSA: I…I don't really feel like talking about it.

HENRY: Char, you know Melissa's doing a painting for the mayor's wife.

CHARLOTTE: It's amazing how far you can go with a hobby, isn't it?

HENRY: Char.

CHARLOTTE: I only mean that persistence pays off. That's all. *(To* MELISSA*)* Where's your fiancé?

HENRY: Jack.

CHARLOTTE: Jack. Yeah. Am I gonna get to meet him?

MELISSA: Oh…he's got a lot on his plate right now…

CHARLOTTE: I'd like to meet him.

MELISSA: Oh, you…you will.

HENRY: You'll like him.

CHARLOTTE: She doesn't have a fiance, Henry.

HENRY: Honey, his name's Jack. I met him. I told you. Remember?

CHARLOTTE: Please. I know my daughter. And she's not engaged. Are you, Melissa?

(No response)

CHARLOTTE: See?

HENRY: What happened? I really liked him. And he really seemed to love you. You could tell by the way he looked at you. I'm sure you'll work things out. Whatever happened.

MELISSA: Dad. *(She looks at them both.)* We were never engaged. I made it up.

(Pause)

HENRY: Oh.

MELISSA: And I was fired from my job. I told Jack I was laid off. But I was really fired because I sent an e-mail to a co-worker bitching out my boss and accidentally copied my boss on the e-mail. So she fired me.

(CHARLOTTE *gives* HENRY *an "I told you so" look.*)

HENRY: Okay. Is there anything else?

MELISSA: The mayor's wife.

HENRY: She didn't commission a painting from you?

(MELISSA *shakes her head.*)

CHARLOTTE: Well, that was obvious.

(HENRY *sighs.*)

HENRY: Anything else?

MELISSA: My apartment. I was two months behind on rent. So…

CHARLOTTE: You're certainly not here out of the goodness of your own heart.

MELISSA: No.

CHARLOTTE: You're here because you have nowhere else to go. You need us, after all.

MELISSA: Yeah. Mom. That's right.

CHARLOTTE: Isn't it better to have it out in the open?

(*No response*)

HENRY: Mel. (*Beat*) Why so many lies?

MELISSA: (*After a beat*) I don't know.

(*A beat*)

(HENRY *brings the now warm soup back to the table. Sets it in front of* CHARLOTTE *and* MELISSA. *Brings his own bowl over. Sits down. The three of them eat their soup in silence.*)

Scene 5

(Lights up on CHARLOTTE *in a bathrobe braiding* MELISSA's *hair.)*

MELISSA: Ow!

CHARLOTTE: Hold still. *(Beat)* Ten years old already.

MELISSA: Ow.

CHARLOTTE: I have to do it tight or it will fall out by the time you get your picture taken.

*(*CHARLOTTE *sprays the braid with hairspray.* MELISSA *coughs.)*

CHARLOTTE: You'll be the prettiest girl in the fifth grade today. Matt Hogan doesn't stand a chance.

MELISSA: Matt Hogan?

CHARLOTTE: Oh honey, don't play dumb. You've written his name all over every one of your notebooks.

MELISSA: Oh yeah. Matt Hogan. He was adorable.

CHARLOTTE: Was? Don't you like him anymore?

MELISSA: I meant 'is.' He is adorable. I love his freckles.

CHARLOTTE: If you ask me, you shouldn't let him know how you really feel. Keep him guessing. Keep your heart closer to your chest. And you'll have him eating out of your hand.

MELISSA: This is the advice you give a ten-year-old?

CHARLOTTE: You don't need to understand now. Just remember to smile for the picture.

MELISSA: Should I smile with or without my teeth showing?

CHARLOTTE: Teeth showing, of course. You're the only girl in your class without braces.

MELISSA: I'm not the only one.

CHARLOTTE: Let me see your smile.

(MELISSA *forces a smile for her* CHARLOTTE.)

CHARLOTTE: *(She goes back to braiding)* Here's a trick. Think of something that makes you laugh just before the picture. That way your eyes will smile too. You want it to look natural. Not forced.

(A few beats of silence. MELISSA *closes her eyes and enjoys it.* HENRY *begins to enter and stops short when he sees* CHARLOTTE *and* MELISSA. *He observes unnoticed.)*

MELISSA: *(To* CHARLOTTE*)* What do you think I should wear for the picture, Mom?

CHARLOTTE: Don't you want to wear the stirrup pants we bought on Saturday?

MELISSA: Oh, yeah. The stirrup pants. I forgot.

CHARLOTTE: You forgot. After begging me to buy them for months? Stirrup pants. What a ridiculous fashion trend.

MELISSA: They're cool, Mom.

CHARLOTTE: That's what you keep saying. *(She sees* HENRY.)

HENRY: *(Now that he's been "discovered")* What's this?

MELISSA: Mom's braiding my hair for picture day.

HENRY: Picture day.

MELISSA: How's it looking, Mom? *(No response)* Mom?

(CHARLOTTE *suddenly stops braiding and lets go of* MELISSA's *hair.)*

MELISSA: Are you done already? How does it look?

(No response)

MELISSA: Mom?

(CHARLOTTE *gets up and exits.* MELISSA *brings her hand to her head to feel the half-finished braid.)*

HENRY: It's two.

MELISSA: Is it?

HENRY: And your mother is still in a bath robe.

MELISSA: She didn't want to get dressed.

HENRY: She can't just lounge around all day in a bathrobe.

MELISSA: Why not?

HENRY: Because. That's not your mother. That's not who she is. And it's your job to help her keep up—

MELISSA: With appearances?

HENRY: I'm not asking you to understand. I'm asking you to cooperate.

MELISSA: Fine.

HENRY: And next time you want to take a trip down memory lane at your mother's expense—

MELISSA: Her expense? She wanted…it was…it helps her.

HENRY: Does it? Or does it help you?

(A beat)

MELISSA: You said the doctor said not to argue with her current reality.

HENRY: Just go get her dressed.

(While MELISSA *is exiting:)*

HENRY: Please.

*(*MELISSA *undoes the braid as she exits leaving* HENRY *on stage.)*

(End of scene)

Scene 6

(Night. The shed. MELISSA *is in the shed/studio staring at her mom's brain scan which sits on the easel when* CHARLOTTE *suddenly enters.)*

MELISSA: What are you doing? *(She hides the brain scan.)*

CHARLOTTE: You haven't been painting. Have you? These are all blank.

MELISSA: Mom, are you...

CHARLOTTE: Perfectly lucid, thank you. *(Short beat)* Why haven't you been painting? You spend enough time in here.

MELISSA: I've been trying.

CHARLOTTE: If you'd been trying, wouldn't there be paint on at least one of these blank canvasses?

MELISSA: Well, it's not easy. It's not like it just happens when you want it to. And sometimes it seems like the harder I try, the harder it is. Why do you care, anyway?

CHARLOTTE: Whatever you choose to do, you should do it well.

(Beat)

MELISSA: Do you want me to run you a bath?

CHARLOTTE: I'm on my way out.

MELISSA: To where?

CHARLOTTE: I told you a hundred times. Book club. And I'm running late.

MELISSA: Well, then I'll run you a bath.

CHARLOTTE: I don't have time for a bath.

MELISSA: Do you have time to brush your hair? Or get dressed?

(A beat)

CHARLOTTE: Where's your father?

MELISSA: At work.

CHARLOTTE: Fine.

MELISSA: Mom, do you think…can you just…can I just have one space of my own?

CHARLOTTE: What's that? Is that my PET scan?

MELISSA: Dad said I could borrow it.

CHARLOTTE: Why?

MELISSA: Do you want me to run you a bath, Mom?

CHARLOTTE: You're going to paint it, aren't you? I am your subject. My brain, rather. My pain. Your art. Is that it?

(No response. Then…)

MELISSA: Let me run you a bath.

CHARLOTTE: I can run my own bath. I'm not a child.

MELISSA: I know.

CHARLOTTE: I want my own space too.

(CHARLOTTE exits. MELISSA looks at the blank canvas. Turns it around)

(End of scene)

Scene 7

(Support group)

(CHARLOTTE sits on a plastic chair center stage, dressed in a blouse, heels and a skirt.)

CHARLOTTE: Laugh and smile. Right? That's what we do. We put others at ease. Somehow that's still a part of me. This desire to put others at ease. Laugh and smile.

Henry, my husband, said it. I'm good at covering. Kept
up the charade for a while. But…

It's like this.

(She stands.)

Being on stage. I feel your eyes like lasers on my skin.
Not just now. All the time.

(She removes her earrings.)

I have this life. Things I've done in my life that were
important to me.

(She removes her scarf.)

I went to great lengths to impress the people in my life.
Appearance. Manners. Decorum. All so important to
me.

(She unbuttons her shirt.)

It's like this. Like living in the midst of a never
ending earthquake where the ground beneath my feet
constantly shifts and threatens to collapse entirely.
Nothing is stable. Things crash around me. I crash
around me. I can't count on the ground to be there. I
can't count on myself to be there…

(She removes her shirt…exposing her bra.)

It's like waking up in a field of poppies with strange
companions in a strange land with no knowledge of
how I got there and no time to get up to speed. I'm just
expected to know how to navigate this new scenario.
That I should know how to survive. That I should at
the very least, recognize it.

(She removes her heels.)

It's like opening a book I've read a million times before
and encountering nothing but unknown territory. My
past is unknown territory.

(She removes her nylons.)

Pictures tell me I've been happy and well traveled.
Pictures tell me I graduated summa cum laude.

Pictures tell me I was a mother. My daughter's
presence tells me that I still am.
*(She removes her skirt. She is now in only her bra and
underwear.)*
It's like this. That nightmare. Showing up to school
naked. Or church. Or the grocery store. Or... support
group. Suddenly I'm naked. This is how I feel every
day of my life. It's not just me, is it? What was I doing?
A bath. Yes. That was it. I think I'll take a bath. A good
soak always...

(CHARLOTTE trails off, exiting. Lights)

Scene 8

*(MELISSA sits on the couch, staring at the floor in front of
her while HENRY paces.)*

(HENRY makes himself a drink. MELISSA watches.)

HENRY: I was never a Bourbon drinker until you were
born. The night you were born I met a former colleague
for a drink at the bar across the street from the hospital.
This colleague, as it happened, also was a father to
a little girl. He wanted to impart some wisdom. He
bought me a glass of Evan Williams twnty-three year-
old bourbon and warned me that my heart would
break over and over again. *(Beat)* He warned me. He
did warn me.
More bourbon.

MELISSA: Mom's fine. She'll be fine. She didn't even
have a concussion.

HENRY: You left her alone.

MELISSA: She was taking a bath. What do you want me
to bathe her now too?

HENRY: You have no room for that tone.

MELISSA: That tone? Dad, this could've happened to anyone.

HENRY: She stepped into a tub of scorching water, fell backwards and hit her head.

MELISSA: How was I supposed to know she wouldn't check the water?

HENRY: I hired you to—

MELISSA: You hired me?

HENRY: Yes. Did I not?

MELISSA: I guess. It's just—

HENRY: You're not living here for fun. Or because you want to. Because you missed us. Wanted to be closer to us. *(Beat)* You're living here for free, not paying rent and—

MELISSA: You want me to pay rent?

HENRY: And I'm paying you. I'm paying you to care for your mother!

MELISSA: You want me to do it for free? Pay rent? What?

HENRY: You have time to paint, but not cook or—

MELISSA: I said I'd make you something.

HENRY: Or clean or… make sure my wife is safe.

MELISSA: *(Beat) Your wife* didn't want my help.

HENRY: Your job is to help.

MELISSA: The last thing she wants is to be treated like a child who can't be left alone. I was just trying to help her maintain some dignity.

HENRY: I need to be able to count on you, Melissa.

MELISSA: So hypocritical.

HENRY: What?

MELISSA: Nothing.

HENRY: Speak up.

MELISSA: You left Mom alone. You let her wander off at night alone. And she almost drowned in Lake Michigan!

HENRY: That was before I knew how bad—

MELISSA: For the owner of a sign company you sure are good at ignoring signs.

HENRY: There were no signs.

MELISSA: There were. There always are. You just didn't want to acknowledge them, so you did what you do best.

HENRY: You think you have all the information?

MELISSA: You pretended everything was fine.

HENRY: If you're no longer happy with this arrangement, I can find someone else to take your place.

MELISSA: Mom doesn't want to be managed. She needs some independence, some how—

HENRY: Hire an actual nurse. Someone who will putt Charlotte's needs first.

MELISSA: Dad...

HENRY: You can go back to your apartment, spend time with...Jack.

MELISSA: You want me out?

HENRY: I shouldn't have expected you to know what to do.

MELISSA: Mom's fine. I mean you're acting like she almost died or something—

HENRY: It could have been so much worse.

MELISSA: But it wasn't—

HENRY: It's not what happened. It's your attitude.

MELISSA: My attitude?

HENRY: Yes. About what happened, about your mom... you're not...you show nothing of...you show nothing.

MELISSA: I show nothing? What is that? You asked me for help and I'm here. I show nothing?!

HENRY: Not a single care for anyone other than yourself.

MELISSA: Then why am I here?

HENRY: I don't know. Do you?

(A long beat)

MELISSA: I shouldn't have left her alone. I'm sorry. You're right. *(She stands.)* I'm gonna check on her.

HENRY: No.

MELISSA: It's been twenty minutes. We're supposed to check every twenty—

HENRY: I'll check. You... Take the night off.

MELISSA: Why?

HENRY: Just take the night off. Please.

(End of scene)

Scene 9

(CHARLOTTE and HENRY's bedroom. CHARLOTTE sits on the bed in her nightgown.)

(HENRY enters and watches her for a beat. He crosses to the dresser and takes off his watch.)

CHARLOTTE: Oh.

HENRY: You okay?

CHARLOTTE: Fine. I just...I just love you in that shirt.

HENRY: How's your head?

CHARLOTTE: You look so handsome.

(HENRY *just looks at himself in the dresser mirror. She crosses to him and begins to unbutton his shirt. He lets her at first, then pulls away.*)

HENRY: It's okay.

CHARLOTTE: What?

HENRY: I'm…it's been a long day. Hasn't it?

CHARLOTTE: I smell bourbon.

HENRY: I'm tired.

CHARLOTTE: Henry…I'm not wearing underwear.

(CHARLOTTE *runs her hands over* HENRY's *white T-shirted chest. She goes to lift the shirt, but he stops her.*)

HENRY: It's cold.

CHARLOTTE: We'll warm each other up.

(CHARLOTTE *takes* HENRY's *hand and pulls him to the bed. She sits him down and rubs his shoulders.*)

CHARLOTTE: How's that?

HENRY: That's nice.

CHARLOTTE: Does it feel good?

HENRY: Yes.

(CHARLOTTE *kisses* HENRY's *neck, then his mouth…then she stops.*)

CHARLOTTE: Henry, come on.

HENRY: You really should rest, Charlotte.

CHARLOTTE: Not yet.

HENRY: It's been a long day.

CHARLOTTE: Henry.

HENRY: We should both rest.

CHARLOTTE: I'm not tired.

HENRY: Well, I am.

(A long beat)

CHARLOTTE: You don't want me?

HENRY: That's not—

CHARLOTTE: I'm so wet, Henry.

HENRY: Charlotte. That's...crass.

CHARLOTTE: God.

HENRY: It doesn't sound like you.

(CHARLOTTE just looks at HENRY.)

HENRY: It's just not you.

CHARLOTTE: Not me?

HENRY: Not that I'm used to.

CHARLOTTE: I'm your wife and I'm...

HENRY: What?

CHARLOTTE: Horny. Henry. Okay? Am I allowed to say that? I'm horny. What are you going to do about it?

(A beat. HENRY does nothing.)

CHARLOTTE: Never mind.

(CHARLOTTE gets in bed under the covers and rolls away from HENRY. He gets in bed next to her and turns off the light.)

Scene 10

(MELISSA sits at a table sketching and drinking bourbon. JACK enters. She doesn't see him at first. He watches her for a beat.)

JACK: As she lives and breathes.

(MELISSA *turns to see* JACK. *She stands.*)

MELISSA: You came.

JACK: Well, I live two doors down...

MELISSA: I didn't want to just appear on your doorstep and, like, ruin your evening or whatever...I thought I'd come here and call you and see if you could just have a drink or...but you're in a suit—

JACK: I have a date.

MELISSA: You have a date.

JACK: I do.

MELISSA: You're going on a date in a suit.

JACK: I went by your apartment.

MELISSA: I don't live there anymore.

JACK: I gathered. A very tall Russian man lives there now with his pet Schnauzer.

MELISSA: We're not supposed to have pets in that building.

JACK: I also called you.

MELISSA: Yeah...

JACK: More than once.

MELISSA: Do you want a drink?

JACK: And texted.

MELISSA: Or do you have to, like, get going on your date or...because I'd really like to buy you a drink.

JACK: What are you drinking?

MELISSA: Bourbon.

JACK: I only have a few minutes.

MELISSA: Come on. Have a drink. Is it a first date? If it's a first date you'll want to have a drink in you.

JACK: Fine. I'll grab a beer. *(He exits off towards the bar.)*

MELISSA: Put it on my tab!

(MELISSA sits. She fingers a pack of smokes while she waits for JACK. He returns with a beer. He sits. She watches him take a sip. Then;)

MELISSA: You didn't put it on my tab, did you?

JACK: No.

MELISSA: I wasn't avoiding you because you cancelled my show. I know that's what you probably think. You probably think that I was just using you to get somewhere with my work and then when you stopped helping me, I cut you off. Like you were of no use to me anymore, so I had no interest in staying in touch. Or whatever. But that's not true. That's not what happened. I don't want you to think that. Because I was thinking…you probably think that and I can't have you thinking that about me. That I'm just a user. Or that I don't give a shit about anybody other than me. That I'm like some selfish prick or something. Or that I "show nothing." Whatever the hell that means, anyway. Because I'm not. I mean. I don't. Or I do. I don't know.

JACK: Yeah.

MELISSA: Yeah what?

JACK: Yeah, that's kind of exactly what I was thinking.

MELISSA: —

JACK: Maybe not after the first call. Or even the second. But after the fifth. And the texts. And then the fact that you moved without even calling me to ask for help. Which is funny. Funny that I was disappointed that I didn't get to help you move your futon and your broken chair and your boxes.

MELISSA: Chair's not broken anymore, remember? You fixed it.

JACK: I did, didn't I? *(He drinks.)*

MELISSA: You were disappointed you didn't get to help me move?

JACK: Fucked up, right? Kind of had me see things more clearly, though.

MELISSA: Things?

JACK: You give me your puppy dog eyes and I'm just happy to do anything for you… to keep those eyes on me. *(Beat)* Was. *(Drinks)*

MELISSA: Okay, maybe that's how I've been from time to time. But, that's not who I am. I mean, I'm a not a user. I don't use people. I didn't use you.

(JACK just stares at MELISSA for a beat. She takes a cigarette out of the case and fingers it.)

JACK: You taking up smoking?

MELISSA: Thinking about it. I used to smoke. And… well, I had a…fight…with my dad. Because I live with my parents now. Which isn't embarrassing at all.

JACK: *(Regarding the sketch pad)* What's this?

(JACK reaches for it and MELISSA pulls it away.)

MELISSA: It's nothing.

JACK: Come on. You're not gonna show me? You always show me your work.

MELISSA: It's nothing.

JACK: You been painting a lot, then? At your parents'?

MELISSA: Yeah. Tons. Feeling really good about my work and—no. I haven't painted anything. I've been completely empty. Stuff's been going on, so it's been hard.

JACK: What kind of stuff?

MELISSA: Just family stuff. Where you taking her? Your date.

JACK: The opera.

MELISSA: The opera?

JACK: Yeah, it's an Italian opera, I don't even know.

MELISSA: You're going on a first date to the opera? In a suit.

JACK: I never said it was a first date.

MELISSA: Oh.

JACK: So, I have to…

MELISSA: Yeah.

(JACK *takes another sip of beer, then stands.*)

JACK: Well, I'm happy to see that you're alive.

MELISSA: Yes, that I am. And thanks for squeezing me in before your fancy date.

JACK: I hope you'll answer next time I call, Melissa.

MELISSA: Oh, you plan to call again. That's great to hear.

JACK: Are you pissed or something?

MELISSA: No. No, why would you think that?

JACK: You seem…you know what. It's not worth it. I have to go.

MELISSA: Wait. Here.

(MELISSA *hands* JACK *a cigarette.*)

JACK: I don't smoke.

MELISSA: I know. Just take it.

JACK: I don't want it.

MELISSA: But I want you to have it. I wanted to buy you a drink and you wouldn't let me. So please just take the cigarette.

(JACK *doesn't.*)

MELISSA: Take it.

JACK: No.

MELISSA: Jack.

JACK: No, thank you.

MELISSA: You can give it to your date after you fuck her.

JACK: Jesus.

MELISSA: Sorry. I don't know…just, please take the cigarette. You can give it to a homeless person or something. Make their night.

(MELISSA *gently places it behind* JACK's *ear. He lets her. She looks at him. A beat*)

MELISSA: Did you mean it? When you said you had faith in me?

JACK: I still do.

(*A beat*)

MELISSA: Well, you should get out of here if you want to make that opera.

JACK: I really don't want to.

MELISSA: Then don't.

(*Lights. End of scene*)

MELISSA: You fell.

CHARLOTTE: I fall now. That's what I do. It's not your fault. *(Beat)* You're painting.

MELISSA: Mom, I'm sorry. I—

CHARLOTTE: Me too. *(A beat)* You know I still have all my teeth.

(MELISSA puts her paint brush down and sits with CHARLOTTE.)

MELISSA: You do. And they're very nice.

CHARLOTTE: That's the problem. I'm attractive and I have all my teeth. People don't expect me to be crazy.

MELISSA: You're not crazy.

CHARLOTTE: At least Grandma had dentures before she started losing her mind. She'd already come to terms with loss of that scale. I mean, you lose your teeth and you've got to face the fact that other parts will follow.

MELISSA: Grandma wore dentures?

CHARLOTTE: I'm losing parts. Little by little.

MELISSA: Better than all at once.

CHARLOTTE: I'll forget you. I'll forget me. I'll become someone else. Maybe even a better version of myself. As if that were possible.

(MELISSA laughs.)

CHARLOTTE: Oh, so it is possible?

MELISSA: Only slightly.

CHARLOTTE: I feel like I'm falling off the map of the world. All alone.

MELISSA: I'll be here.

Charlotte holds Melissa in her gaze.

MELISSA: If…if you want me to be. If Dad wants me to be.

(CHARLOTTE *gets up and crosses to* MELISSA'*s painting.*)

MELISSA: It's not finished. I—

CHARLOTTE: You did this last night?

MELISSA: I haven't slept.

CHARLOTTE: It's…

MELISSA: I hope it's okay.

CHARLOTTE: *That's* how it feels.

(MELISSA *just looks at* CHARLOTTE. *A beat*)

CHARLOTTE: You can really paint.

(MELISSA *hugs* CHARLOTTE.)

CHARLOTTE: Honey, can I ask you a favor?

MELISSA: Of course.

CHARLOTTE: I know you're busy, but do you think you might be able to stay with us for a little bit? Just a couple of weeks. For your dad's sake. He's been really down. I'm not sure why, but I think you being here would cheer him up. I know it's a lot to ask.

(MELISSA *just nods.*)

CHARLOTTE: Okay. Good.

(*A beat.* CHARLOTTE *stares at the painting again.*)

MELISSA: Want some coffee? I could make some.

CHARLOTTE: No. Just finish it. You paint. I'll watch. Okay?

MELISSA: Okay.

CHARLOTTE: Okay.

(*As* MELISSA *paints, the light slowly fades out on* CHARLOTTE.)

(MELISSA turns around. CHARLOTTE is gone.)

MELISSA: Mom?

(Lights)

END OF PLAY

Scene 12

(CHARLOTTE *and* HENRY's *bedroom. They are both in bed. She, sleeping; he, thinking.*)

(*He holds an old photo album in his lap. He opens the album....*)

(*Photos of* HENRY *and* CHARLOTTE *on their wedding day, on their honeymoon... He stops at a picture of her that he particularly loves.*)

(*He's seized by a sudden attack of emotion. He tries to choke it back. But can't.*)

(CHARLOTTE *stirs. She rolls over and sits up.*)

HENRY: (*Wiping his tears away*) I'm sorry...I didn't mean...

(CHARLOTTE *takes the photo album from* HENRY *and closes it. She puts it aside. She looks at him like she's never seen him before. He searches for something in her eyes.*)

(*She takes him in her arms and holds him while he cries.*)

Scene 13

(*Morning*)

(*Lights up on* MELISSA *in the shed. Painting. In the same clothes from the night before.* CHARLOTTE *enters in her nightgown.*)

MELISSA: Mom?

(CHARLOTTE *touches* MELISSA's *head.*)

MELISSA: How's your head?

CHARLOTTE: I can't remember.

MELISSA: It was my fault.

CHARLOTTE: What was your fault?